DIFFERENT IS BEAUTIFUL

WHO chains YOU.com PUBLISHING

PENELOPE LAGOS

ILLUSTRATED BY
CHARLES BERTON

Published by Who Chains You Books
P.O. Box 581
Amissville, VA 20106
WhoChainsYou.com

Written by Penelope Lagos
penelopelagos.com

Illustrated by Charles Berton
CharlesBerton.com

Cover and Interior design by Tamira Thayne
tamirathayne.com

ISBN: 978-1-946044-82-2

Printed in the United States of America

First Edition

DEDICATION

In Loving Memory of my best friend,
Cassius "The Legend" Lagos.

This book is written for all of the animals
and humans who are perfectly imperfect. ♡

*Penelope
+
Cassius*

"**W**ake up, look alive, everyone! Today is the big day," Cassius shouted.

"Shhh, we're trying to get our beauty sleep!" Satchmo grumbled.

"No time for sleep, Satchmo," Cassius barked. "It's the annual Paws 'n Claws Adoption Day. The biggest event of the year. If we have any chance of getting out of these cages, we need to be alert now and plan our strategy."

"Do you think we have a chance of finding a home?" Satchmo said. Satchmo was a large silver-grey poodle who had diabetes and needed a lot of care. "At the last event, none of us got adopted. A lot of people were calling us special needs. I guess that's a bad thing?"

"It's not a bad thing, and today we're going to turn that thinking around," Cassius announced.

"I hope we can," Kelly exclaimed. "I always knew I could only see from one eye, but none of you ever treated me differently. Why do humans?"

"We have to remind them," Paco squawked as he hobbled to the front of his cage.

"We will teach by example," Peanut, a beautiful cat chimed in. Hopper, the runt of his litter, rounded the corner on his wheels and nodded in agreement.

While everyone was talking, Spike, a very smart, handsome, and deaf Jack Russell Terrier looked up from his dog bowl. Even though the little guy couldn't hear his friends, he sensed what was going on.

"I want to stay positive, but even the volunteers separated us from the rest of the shelter," an all-black cat named Gabby added. "Let's face it," she said, "we don't fit in. We are different."

All the animals began to talk at once and the room filled with noise.

Cassius raised his voice and said, "Listen up, we need to join together and work as a team. If we work hard, we can change people's thinking. Who's with me?" Paco chirped in approval and one by one the others followed.

After a few minutes, the volunteers started walking in potential new families. Cassius showed off his great big smile.

"Mom," one child shouted, "he looks like a pirate. I want him."

The woman turned to the volunteer and whispered, "Is he a pitbull?"

"Yes," the volunteer hesitated.

The woman leaned down to her daughter and said, "We will find another dog."

Cassius had heard this many times before, but this time he wouldn't let it get him down. Gabby was told black cats were for witches. Kelly heard one-eyed cats don't have balance and could no longer play.

Someone looked at Paco and said, "Awww, he only has one leg, how sad." The animals had always treated everyone at the shelter the same; now they wanted the humans to treat them the same too.

"Stay positive," Cassius mouthed to Spike.

As the end of the event neared, the last to arrive was a little boy named George and his father, Harry. George immediately noticed Cassius and yelled out, "Dad, come here. Look at this dog. I love him."

Cassius licked the boy's hand and raised his paw for a high five.

"Excuse me," Harry turned to one of the volunteers. "How old is this dog?"

"**W**ell, he answered, "Cassius has been with us for quite some time now. He's a senior, so we believe he is eight years old."

"NO!" Cassius screamed in his head. "You'll ruin this for me by calling me a senior . . . I can do all the same things a puppy can!"

"I'm sorry, Son," George's father replied, "he's just too old. We're looking for a younger dog."

George fought back his tears and pleaded,
"But Dad. He's perfect, and he loves me too."
Cassius continued to lick his hand.

The boy persisted, "Ever since Mom's accident,
you told me the other kids at school might think
I'm different because mom is in a wheelchair."

"I know, Son," Harry responded,
"but that's different."

"It's not different, Dad. We are all unique, even animals. Mom always told me to treat others the way I want to be treated. She told me we may look different on the outside, but we are the same inside. Cassius isn't a puppy, but he has the same love to give that a puppy does."

Harry turned to his son and remarked, "You are very wise for your age, do you know that?"

George nodded, "We learned in school that different is beautiful. I think Cassius is very different, AND he's beautiful, too."

"As do I, Son."

Harry talked to the volunteer to learn more about Cassius and make sure he would be a good fit for their family. Then he leaned down to Cassius and said, smiling, "Welcome to the family, good boy!"

As Cassius proudly trotted off with his new family, he stopped and turned to wink at the others. They all returned his smile, knowing that if they followed in Cassius' footsteps, they would all be fine, too.

THE END

Tips for Learning Not to Judge Others

1. Lead by example. Monitor your thoughts.
   Judging others defines who you are, not who they are.
2. Look for the positive. Judgments are negative.
3. Pause before you speak. Will your words hurt
   another person?
4. Look for the good in everyone.
5. Engage in random acts of kindness.
6. Have open conversations with your child about the
   stereotypes and bias that exist around the world.
7. Expose your child to diverse/multicultural experiences
   and all walks of life.
8. Educate yourself and your child. Outward appearances
   don't define who we are.
9. Avoid judgmental language.
10. Be kind, spread love and don't forget to smile.
    It's contagious!

Love the book? Please consider giving **DIFFERENT IS BEAUTIFUL** a review on Amazon and other venues. Your reviews mean the world to our authors. *Thank you!*

About the Author

Penelope Lagos, a New Jersey native, graduated from Rutgers University with a BA in Communications and Theatre Arts. Penelope is an avid animal advocate and strongly believes in being "a voice for the voiceless." She holds certifications in Canine Fitness and Conditioning as well as Advanced Pet CPR/First Aid. She is the recipient of the Reader's Favorite 5 star award for her first children's book entitled *I Miss My Best Friend,* which deals with the grief of losing a pet. When Penelope is not spending time with her own furry friends, she is acting in indie films and commercials as well as volunteering at The Leukemia and Lymphoma Society (LLS). Penelope is the recipient of the LLS Achievement Award for her dedication in fundraising events.

About the Illustrator

Charles Berton is the illustrator of a wide array of children's books, as well as many book covers, posters and anything on or in which one can have illustrations. He had a natural inclination to draw from the age of five. As an adult, he was trained and certified in web and graphic design. He raised a family on Long Island where he was also born and raised, and where he continues to live and work today. Feel free to visit CharlesBerton.com and see many samples of his work and philosophy.

About Who Chains You Books

At Who Chains You, we publish books for those who believe people—and animals—deserve to be free

Who Chains You Publishing brings you books that educate, entertain, and share gripping plights of the animals we serve and those who rescue and stand in their stead.

We offer all kinds of stories about all kinds of animals: dogs, cats, rats, cows, pigeons, horses, pigs, snails, squirrels, chickens, and many more to come! *Visit our site and read more about us at www.whochainsyou.com.*

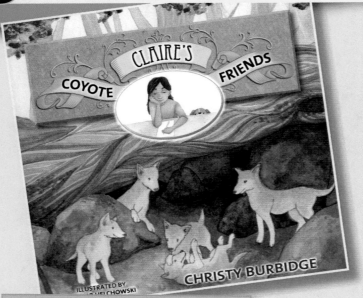

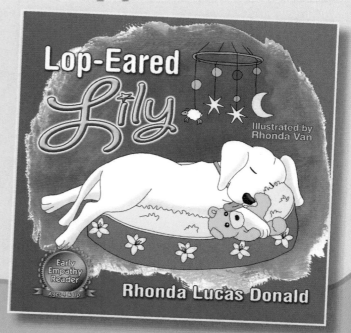

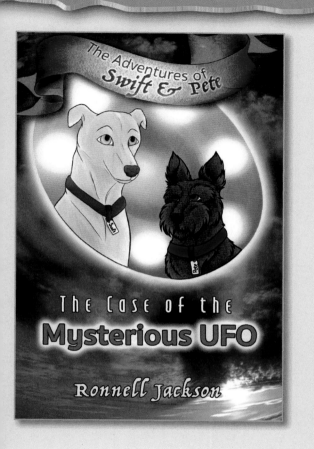

The Adventures of Swift & Pete

The Case of the Mysterious UFO

Ronnell Jackson

Samantha K. Riggi

The Sleepy Honey Bee

Illustrated by Rhonda Van

WHO Chains YOU.com PUBLISHING

Squeak THE Squirrel

WRITTEN & ILLUSTRATED BY Rhonda Van

Made in the USA
Middletown, DE
15 September 2020